Sports Illustrated KIDS

BIG-TIME RECORDS

BIG-TIME
EXTREME SPORTS RECORDS

BY DREW LYON

D0103065

CAPSTONE PRESS
a capstone imprint

Published by Capstone Press, an imprint of Capstone.
1710 Roe Crest Drive
North Mankato, Minnesota 56003
capstonepub.com

Library of Congress Cataloging-in-Publication Data
Names: Lyon, Drew, author.
Title: Big-time extreme sports records / by Drew Lyon.
Description: North Mankato, Minnesota : Capstone Press, 2022. | Series: Sports illustrated kids big-time records | Includes bibliographical references. | Audience: Ages 8–11 |
   Audience: Grades 4–6
Identifiers: LCCN 2021004162 (print) | LCCN 2021004163 (ebook) | ISBN 9781496695499
   (hardcover) | ISBN 9781977158963 (paperback) | ISBN 9781977158970 (ebook PDF)
Subjects: LCSH: Extreme sports—Records—Juvenile literature.
Classification: LCC GV749.7 .L96 2022 (print) | LCC GV749.7 (ebook) | DDC 796.04/6—dc23
LC record available at https://lccn.loc.gov/2021004162
LC ebook record available at https://lccn.loc.gov/2021004163

Summary: WHOOSH! Nothing beats the excitement of an extreme athlete launching high into the air—except when that big stunt sets a new record! Behind every big-time record is a dramatic story of how an athlete achieved greatness in his or her sport. Strap on your pads, grab your helmet, and read all about the greatest awe-inspiring and record-setting achievements by the world's most extreme athletes.

Editorial Credits
Editor, Aaron Sautter; Designer, Bobbie Nuytten; Media Researcher, Morgan Walters; Production Specialist, Laura Manthe

Image Credits
Alamy: AF archive, 9, TCD/Prod.DB, 17; Associated Press: Christian Pondella, 7, Ramon Espinosa, 33, Valentin Luthiger, 15; Getty Images: Bettmann, 5, Christian Pondella, 25, Icon Sports Wire, 61; Bottom of Form, Phil Walter, 11, RacingOne, 21, Richard Bord, 31, Shaun Botterill, 59, Stefan Matzke - sampics, 43, Tim Clayton - Corbis, 49; Newscom: Bob Hallinen/ZUMA Press, 53, Icon SMI/Marc Piscotty, Cover, imageSPACE/Sipa USA, 50, Lynn Wegener/ZUMA Press, 55, Mike Isler/Icon SMI, 35, Pierre Tostee/ZUMAPRESS, 41, Red Bull/ZUMAPRESS, 29, Roland Harrison/Action Plus, 47, Steve Boyle/ZUMAPRESS, 19, Tony Donaldson/Icon SMI, 23, 27, 45, VUE Images/Red Bull/SIPA, 13 ; Shutterstock: alysta, 37, shubhamtiwari, 51; Sports Illustrated: Robert Beck, 39, Simon Bruty, 57

All records and statistics in this book are current through 2020.

TABLE OF CONTENTS

WORDS IN **BOLD** APPEAR IN THE GLOSSARY.

EXTREME MEASURES

The history of extreme sports can be divided into two chapters—before Evel Knievel and after Evel Knievel. The daredevil opened imaginations, bringing alternative sports into America's living rooms. During his career, Knievel attempted over 75 ramp-to-ramp motorcycle jumps.

Robert Knievel starred in traditional sports in high school. In the 1960s he changed his name and pursued a career as a motorcycle stunt artist. In 1965 Knievel tried jumping over a 90-foot (27-meter) long box filled with rattlesnakes and two mountain lions. He nearly landed on the rattlesnakes. Later, he attempted to clear 12 cars and a cargo van. Knievel crashed and broke several bones.

"People don't come to see me die," he said. "They come to see me defy death."

In 1971 he cleared a record 19 cars across 129 feet (39 m). In 1974 he launched, literally, his boldest stunt. Riding in a steam-powered rocket, he tried flying across the Snake River Canyon in Idaho. However, the rocket's parachute opened upon take-off. Instead of flying across the canyon, the rocket fell slowly to the canyon floor. Still, Knievel received an E for Effort.

"I did everything by the seat of my pants," he said. "That's why I got hurt so much."

Evel Knievel Records

Guinness Book of World Records: most bones broken in a lifetime (estimated: 433)

Most cars jumped (19); record was broken in 1998 by Bubba Blackwell (20)

Evel Knievel successfully jumped over 19 cars on February 28, 1971, at Ontario Motor Speedway in California.

Like Father, Like Son

Evel's son, Robbie Knievel, followed in his father's footsteps. Robbie has repeated many of Evel's tricks, including a 228-foot (69.5-m) jump off part of the Grand Canyon. In tribute to his father, Robbie wears a similar red, white, and blue jumpsuit during his stunts.

THE AIR UP THERE

Miles Above

June 19, 2017, landed on the eve of the summer solstice. It was one of the year's longest days. **BASE** jumper Miles Daisher had 24 hours to regain the record for most unassisted jumps in one day. His previous record of 57 jumps had been topped by Danny Weiland. Daisher aimed to reclaim the record.

Shortly after 10 a.m., Daisher took his first leap off the I.B. Perrine Bridge in his hometown of Twin Falls, Idaho. After each landing, Daisher climbed 486 feet (148 m) back up the rocky cliffs before making another jump. By the next morning, Daisher set a record with 63 jumps. In 24 hours Daisher climbed a total of 30,618 feet (9,332 m). That's higher than Mount Everest, the world's tallest mountain!

But Daisher's record didn't last long. Three months later, Weiland completed jump number 64 in less than 24 hours. He had three hours left to pad his total. But Weiland didn't need to pile on.

Daisher has attempted more than 5,000 BASE jumps during his 25-year career. He's also the inventor of skyaking and rope swing BASE jumps.

Most Unassisted Jumps in 24 Hours

Danny Weiland: 64 (Sept. 17, 2017)

Miles Daisher: 63 (June 20, 2017)

Danny Weiland: 61 (2016)

Miles Daisher: 57 (2005)

Daisher BASE jumped off a bridge in Twin Falls, Idaho, a record 63 times on June 19, 2017.

"I don't look at (Miles) as a rival," he said, "I look at him as a brother."

While thrilling, **aerial** sports are also dangerous. Every leap comes with a risk. No one should BASE jump without proper training, even record-breakers.

"Base jumping is probably the deadliest sport in the world," wrote BASE jumper Chris McNamara. "It is also probably the coolest."

Jump for Joy

National Guardsman Dan Schilling jumped off Idaho's Perrine Bridge a record 201 times in 24 hours. However, his record is considered "assisted" because each time he jumped into the Snake River Gorge, a huge crane brought him back up. He was also aided by a team of parachute packers.

The Danger Zone

Videographer Carl Boenish was considered "the father of BASE jumping." Boenish took extreme flying to the next level, and filmed his revolution. Boenish parachuted off planes 1,500 times.

In 1978 Boenish brought a team of skydivers to the El Capitan cliffs in Yosemite National Park. With cameras rolling 3,000 feet (914 m) above ground, Boenish and his team jumped. They descended at speeds exceeding 100 miles (161 kilometers) per hour before opening their chutes and landing safely. A new extreme sport and filmmaking style were born. Boenish later set a record when he made a successful 6,000-foot (1,829-m) jump.

Boenish said BASE jumping made him feel like Superman. But this Superman wasn't superhuman. In 1984 Boenish's life and career ended in tragedy. He died in a jumping accident in Norway. Two days later, Carl's wife, Jean, honored her late husband by jumping from the same site where Carl made his final successful jump. His legacy, films, and the sport he created live on today.

"(Carl) loved expanding the sense of the possible," Jean said.

In 1980 the U.S. government banned BASE jumping off El Capitan.

Highest BASE Jumping Elevation

Valery Rozov jumped from Mount Everest, 23,687 feet (7,220 meters), or about 4.5 miles, above sea level.

Footage from the 2014 film *Sunshine Superman*, a movie about Boenish's life, showed him BASE jumping from a tall building.

Bungee Man

A.J. Hackett didn't invent **bungee jumping,** but he is the sport's most extreme promoter. Bungee jumping began as an ancient South Pacific ritual called "land diving." Young native men tied vines to their ankles and jumped off a high wooden tower to prove their manhood.

The Pacific islanders' ritual inspired Hackett. He decided to try jumping using rubber cords. But before jumping, he needed to know the bungee rubber was strong enough. Hackett made his first jump from a 19-foot (5.8-m) bridge. The rubber cord passed the test.

In 1987 he forged a bold plan. Driving around Paris, Hackett decided to jump from the Eiffel Tower. He leaped from the building with a view that few, if any, humans had seen. Hackett's dangerous jump inspired millions to take the plunge.

Bungee Jumping World Records by A.J. Hackett

1. 1988: World's first bungee jump off the Auckland Stock Exchange Tower
2. 1990: First bungee jump from a helicopter at 1,247 feet (380 m)
3. 2000: Jumped from the world's highest suspension bridge
4. 2006: Highest bungee jump off a building, Macau Tower in Macau, China, 764 feet (233 m)
5. 2015: Most people bungee jumping in 24 hours: 542

Hackett set numerous records, including the first jump from a helicopter. His most recent record involved hundreds of bungee jumpers. To celebrate the 25th anniversary of Hackett's jumping business, 541 jumpers joined him. Using 19,570 feet (5,965 m) of bungee cord, Hackett's crew beat the record by 36 people.

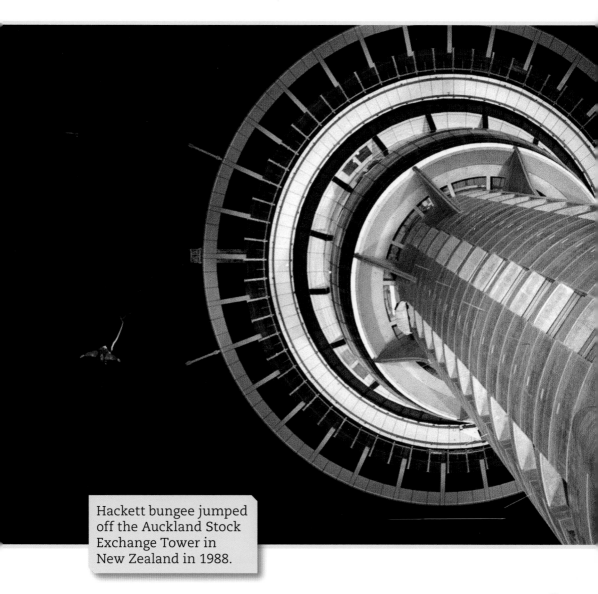

Hackett bungee jumped off the Auckland Stock Exchange Tower in New Zealand in 1988.

Hanging Out

In 2012 Jonny Durand and his buddy, Dustin Martin, engaged in a high-stakes duel in the friendly skies. The hang gliders attempted to break the hang gliding distance record. The record of 435 miles (700 km) hadn't been broken in more than ten years. Once the two took off in the air, their friendship was on pause.

To stay in the air, hang gliders rely on **thermals.** Durand and Martin stayed close together in their gliders for about 11 hours. At one point, they flew wingtip to wingtip. Toward the end, Martin caught a thermal and overtook his pal. Martin gained an extra 300 feet (91.4 m) of lift, just enough to soar 3 miles (4.8 km) past Durand. Both broke the record. But Martin claimed the top spot by flying a total of 474.7 miles (764 km).

Durand was happy for Martin—for a while. Four years later, he tried to beat Martin's record on the same path but was denied. He fell short again in 2018. Some records don't fall so easily.

"It's a world record for a reason," Durand said. "It's not easy to break."

Altitude Record for Balloon-Launched Glider

Judy Leden: 38,000 feet (11,582 m). Six months later, Leden broke the World Hang Gliding Altitude Record after being towed to 41,307 feet (12,590 m) by a hot air balloon.

Dustin Martin World Record

Longest Open Distance Flight: 474.7 miles (764 km)

Johnny Durand World Records

Fastest to complete 300-km (186-mile) flight: 4 hours, 16 minutes

Fastest average speed over 100 km (62 miles): 90 kph (56 mph); peak speed: 110 kph (68 mph)

Durand and Australian racing driver Craig Lowndes sailed through the sky over Townsville, Australia, on June 3, 2014.

Climbing to the Top

In 2019 Dani Arnold began climbing the 1,800-foot (549-m) Cima Grande wall in Italy. He had all the necessary equipment—except for a safety rope. That was by choice, though. Arnold stayed in the present while keeping calm and climbing on. After 46 minutes and 30 seconds, he stood victorious. Arnold had completed the fastest **free solo** climb of the Cima Grande. He crushed the previous record by nearly 20 minutes.

Arnold knows the stakes are high when he's free climbing. But he tries not to look too far into the future. Nor does he look below. "I'm very in the moment," he said.

Arnold spends about 200 days a year planning and training for solo climbs. He owns free solo climbing speed records across Europe. He grabbed his first solo speed record on the north face of Mount Eiger in Switzerland. He also set a speed climbing record in Alaska.

After setting his record on the Cima Grande, Arnold was filled with joy—and relief. "I was just happy to stop and (see) that the Cima Grande was not higher," he said.

Dani Arnold Records

Holds speed record on four of Europe's six major north faces

Fastest to climb the Matterhorn mountain in Switzerland: 14,692 feet (4,478 m) in 1 hour 46 minutes, breaking previous record by 10 minutes

Arnold made his way up the icy "Beta Block Super" in Switzerland during a free solo climb in December 2017.

Solo Act

Solo rock climbing is risky business. The climber scales high elevations with neither rope nor safety net. But Alex Honnold doesn't give in to fear. Honnold has completed over 1,000 free solo climbs and set world records at death-defying heights. Yet he manages to keep his cool when his life hangs in the balance.

One climb stood high on Honnold's bucket list. El Capitan in Yosemite National Park stands 3,600 feet (1,100 m) straight up and is made of sheer granite. Honnold had climbed El Capitan 40 times, but never free soloed. Nobody had.

In 2017 Honnold put his training to the test. In less than four hours, he set a record once thought unthinkable. He climbed into history by conquering El Capitan with no ropes or other equipment.

"(Climbing) is when he feels most alive," said his mom, Dierdre Wolownick.

His record is one of the greatest achievements not just in extreme sports, but in any sport. Honnold's fame grew when *Free Solo*, a documentary film about his climb, won an Academy Award.

Alex Honnold Records

Only athlete to free solo El Capitan

Holds speed record for climbing The Nose of El Capitan

Quickest climb (with Tommy Caldwell) of the Yosemite Triple Crown (Mt. Watkins, El Capitan, and Half Dome)

In 2017 Alex Honnold became the first person to free solo the famous El Capitan wall in California.

Alex Honnold isn't the only member of his family to hold climbing records. His mother, Dierdre Wolownick, is the oldest woman to climb El Capitan.

ROLL ON

The GOAT

Motocross legend Ricky Carmichael earned the nickname the GOAT, or Greatest Of All Time, for good reason. Despite his small size, he left his opponents in the dust.

Carmichael's love of motorsports began when his parents gave him a three-wheeler when he was just 5 years old. He went to his first **supercross** race when he was eight. Carmichael saw his future on the racetrack.

His mom, Jeannie, always had Ricky's back. She drove him from Florida to Texas for racing tournaments. He crushed the competition, winning 67 **amateur** titles. Little Carmichael was a giant among the big boys.

His pro career began with three American Motorcyclist Association (AMA) Motocross Championships. He then moved to the 250cc division. He rode a bigger bike, but Carmichael kept winning. For nearly a decade, Carmichael won every national Motocross championship and five supercross titles. He retired from professional motorsports with a record 150 total wins and three X Games gold medals.

He next turned to a career in professional stock racing. In 2010 he started a racing academy to build the next generation of GOATs. All the while, Ricky Carmichael never forgot his roots.

"I'm just a little kid from Florida who could ride a motorcycle," he said.

Carmichael whipped around a tight curve during the AMA Toyota Motocross Championship on July 16, 2006, in New Berlin, New York.

Most AMA Motocross Championships 450/250cc Class

Ricky Carmichael: 7

Ryan Dungey: 3

Jeff Stanton: 3

Ricky Johnson 3

Tony DiStefano: 3

Most AMA Motocross wins 450/250cc Class

Ricky Carmichael: 76

Ryan Dungey: 39

Bob Hannah: 27

Eli Tomac: 23

Ricky Johnson: 22

The King

Ricky Carmichael is the GOAT in motocross. But his childhood idol, Jeremy McGrath, lays claim to the "King of Supercross."

McGrath starred in BMX riding before moving to motor racing. His experience in BMX influenced how he rode in motocross. His cutting-edge style transformed motor biking. During a nearly 20-year career, McGrath sped to the top of the sport's charts. He became the first supercross racer to win the championship in his rookie season.

McGrath's skills made him virtually unbeatable, earning him the nickname "Showtime." The King won seven AMA Supercross Championships, nine straight seasons with an AMA win, two world championships, four X Games medals, and a record 101 overall career wins. He retired with 72 Supercross 450/250cc titles.

"There's no better way to win a championship than dominating," McGrath said.

McGrath remains a popular figure in motocross. He still rides his dirt bike. He also owns his own toy line and a line of sneakers. He's been featured in video games and is a best-selling author. For Jeremy McGrath, it pays to finish first.

Jeremy McGrath Records

- Member of Motorcycle and BMX Halls of Fame
- 12 total championships
- 7 Supercross titles
- 101 career wins
- 4 X Games medals

McGrath rose his arms in victory as he won first place at the Daytona Supercross by Honda on March 6, 1999.

The Birdman

At the 1999 X Games, skateboarder Tony "The Birdman" Hawk tried 10 times to land the first ever 900 trick. He fell short every time. Hawk had already spent ten years trying to complete the difficult trick. He wasn't sure how many more tries he could devote to landing it.

In 1985 Hawk was the first skater to land a 720. But the 900 was just beyond his reach. Hawk had the battle scars to prove it. His past attempts left him with cracked ribs, concussions, and broken teeth.

At the X Games, Hawk kept expectations to a minimum. But he wasn't about to give up. The 11th time was the charm. Hawk launched into the air, spun around 2 1/2 times, and finally landed the 900. Hawk looked shocked as the crowd mobbed him. The Birdman had soared once more.

"This is the best day of my life!" Hawk said.

First 5 Skateboarders to Land a 900

1. Tony Hawk, June 27, 1999, X Games, San Francisco, California

2. Giorgio Zattoni, April 2004, Marianna HC, Ravenna, Italy

3. Sandro Dias, May 2004, Latin X Games, Rio de Janeiro, Brazil

4. Alex Perelson, July 2009, Maloof Money Cup, Costa Mesa, California

5. Bob Burnquist, August 2010, Mega Ramp, Vista, California

Hawk's records inspired generations of skateboarders. YouTube clips of his successful 900s have earned more than 15 million views. More than 20 years later, Hawk's first 900 remains a defining moment in skateboarding.

Tony Hawk caught big air during a trick at the 1999 X Games in San Francisco, California.

Tommy Boy

Tony Hawk probably never thought his 900 achievement would be outdone by a preteen skater. But in 2011, 11-year old phenom Tom Schaar rode a mega ramp to set the record as the youngest skater to land a 900. The 900 was only the beginning for Schaar. He later completed the first documented 1080 in skateboard history. It took him about five tries to complete 3 full spins and land successfully.

"It was the hardest trick I've ever done," Schaar said, "but it was easier than I thought."

Schaar's feat wasn't a fluke. He repeated the trick at the 2012 X Games Shanghai to win the gold medal at age 12 and won gold again in 2014. As he grew older and bigger, it became physically difficult for Schaar to nail a 1080. But he continued skateboarding, and in 2020 he earned a spot on the U.S. Olympic team. Skateboarding keeps Schaar feeling joyful and free, no matter his age.

In May 2020, 11-year old Brazilian skater Gui Khury became the first skateboarder to land a 1080-degree turn on a vertical ramp.

24

Schaar flipped upside down during a trick at the Skateboard Big Air Finals at the 2012 X Games in Los Angeles, California.

The Father of Big Air

Mat Hoffman races with the motto, "Dream big, go big." Inspired by his idol, Evel Knievel, Hoffman pushed the limits in BMX. He only performed for the love of "big air." In 1989 he landed the first 900 in BMX.

His next mission was to fly at least 30 feet (9.1 m) in the air. In 1993 Hoffman went for his most ambitious trick on a 21-foot (6.4-m) high quarter pipe. But he fell hard on one of his runs and was seriously injured. He spent more than a year recovering.

But he still wanted to achieve his dream. In 2001 he made another attempt. With a motorcycle towing him for speed, Hoffman flew 26 feet, 6 inches (8.1 m) high off the quarter pipe. He didn't hit his goal, but he was happy to get the big air record. Later at the 2001 X Games, Mat Hoffman cemented his legend when he landed the first no-handed 900.

"(A)ll you need is a dream and a will, and you can achieve anything," he said.

> **Kevin Robinson, Hoffman's friend, barely broke the BMX big air record in 2008. He bested Hoffman's height by just one inch.**

Highest Jump on a BMX Bike
Kevin Robinson: 26 feet, 7 inches (8.10 m)
Mat Hoffman: 26 feet, 6 inches (8.07 m)

Hoffman spinned his bike for a big trick during the ESPN X Games BMX competition in San Francisco, California, in 1999.

Taking It to the Max

Mountain biker Markus "Max" Stöckl has the need for speed. Using standard, store-bought bikes, he throws caution to the wind. But he also knows that he puts his life in danger each time he rides at high speeds.

In 1999 Stöckl set his first world record. He raced 116 miles (187 km) per hour down a snow-packed hill. Biking at more than 100 miles (161 km) per hour down a snowy hill may be scary for most. But Stöckl believes it's not as dangerous as it seems.

In 2007, sitting atop a 1 mile- (1.6 km-) long slope at a 45-degree slant in Chile, Stöckl was ready to set a new record. He reached a breathtaking speed of 130.7 miles (210 km) per hour. But he wasn't done. He etched his name in history a few years later. In 2011 he shot 3,900 feet (1,189 m) down the side of a volcano, hitting a maximum speed of 102 miles (164 km) per hour. When it comes to mountain biking speed, Stöckl sets the standard.

"If you want to reach a certain goal, then you have to put it all in," he said.

Mountain Bike Speed Records

Flat surface (motor-assisted bike):
Denise Mueller-Korenek, 183.9 mph (296 kph), 2018

Flat surface (motor-assisted bike):
Fred Rompelberg, 167.05 mph (268.8 kph), 1995

Downhill on snow (standard bike):
Markus Stöckl, 130.7 mph (210 kph), 2007

Downhill on gravel (standard bike):
Markus Stöckl, 104.1 mph (167.5 kph), 2017

Markus Stöckl raced down the Cerro Negro volcano in Nicaragua to set a new speed record in May 2011.

It's All Downhill from Here

A devastating crash in 2002 nearly ended the life of extreme biker Eric Barone. The Frenchman was attempting a downhill speed record, hitting a speed of 107 miles (172 km) per hour. Then disaster struck. Barone's **prototype** bike broke and he crashed on the side of a rocky volcano. Barone tore his shoulders and broke bones. His protective equipment likely saved his life.

Barone stepped away from racing for a decade. He rebuilt his body and mind. But his hunger for speed proved too tempting. He had unfinished business.

By 2017 Barone was back in action. After eight months of training, he aimed for another record. Outfitted in protective gear, Barone looked over the snow track, ready to be propelled into history.

His team and fans cheered him on as Barone sped down the mountain in the frigid mountain air. At speeds of 141.5 miles (227.7 km) per hour, Barone broke his previous record. That's faster than most regular cars can drive! Barone was in disbelief. He retired on top of the mountain bike world.

"I couldn't believe it myself. . . . What a great ending to a career," he said.

Eric Barone Records

Downhill on snow (prototype bike):
141.5 mph (227.7 kph)

Downhill on gravel (prototype bike):
107 mph (172 kph)

Barone hurtled down a snowy mountain to set the world speed record in Vars, France, on March 18, 2017.

WATER GAMES

Can't Stop, Won't Stop

Neither the painful sting of jellyfish nor the threat of sharks prevented **endurance** swimmer Chloë McCardel from pursuing glory. In 2013, she attempted a 103-mile (165.8-km) swim from Cuba to Florida. However, after 11 hours, the jellyfish stings were too much to bear.

The Australian came back to overcome the elements in 2014. She swam 77 miles (124 km) for nearly 42 hours in the Bahamas. Battling exhaustion, dehydration, sunburn, and more jellyfish stings, McCardel set the record for the world's longest unassisted ocean swim. To qualify as an unassisted open water swim, McCardel followed English Channel guidelines. She couldn't use protective suits or cages. She could only use her swimsuit, earplugs, goggles, a swim cap, and petroleum jelly.

McCardel holds the world record for most crossings of the English Channel in one season (8), and in one week (3). She's completed 31 crossings and has taught dozens of swimmers to cross the Channel.

"I've pushed myself as much as I thought I could have," she said. "Now, it's about pushing the boundaries of marathon swimming."

Chloë McCardel Records

Longest unassisted ocean swim: 42 hours, 77 miles (124 km)

Youngest member of International Marathon Swimming Hall of Fame

Chloë McCardel wore a protective swim cap and goggles for her record-setting swim from Havana, Cuba, to Florida.

Sarah Thomas World Records

2019: First swimmer to cross the English Channel four times non-stop

2017: Swam 104.6 miles (168.3 km) in Lake Champlain, the first current-neutral open water swim of over 100 miles (161 km)

2016: longest unassisted open water swim, 82 miles (132 km)

Great Lengths

Sarah Thomas holds several swimming records. But in 2017 she found herself in the most important race of all when she was diagnosed with breast cancer. She didn't let it stop her from achieving her dreams. After surviving her cancer fight, in 2019 she became the first swimmer to cross the English Channel four times non-stop. After 54 hours and swimming 84 miles (135 km) in the cold Channel, Thomas proved her toughness held no boundaries.

A Wake in the Parks

Parks Bonifay rode on water before he could even walk. His dad, Pete, put Parks into a pair of water skis at just six months old. Until 2016, Parks held the record for the youngest person to water ski. By the age of 12, Bonifay traded his skis for a wakeboard. He found wakeboarding attractive because of its mobility. He wanted to do flips and jump higher in the water. Wakeboarding made perfecting these tricks easier.

At age 14, Bonifay entered the 1996 X Games. He competed against his idols and won the gold medal. In 1999 Bonifay became the first wakeboarder to land a switch toeside 1080. Before long he perfected more tricks and started naming them.

During his 20-year career, Bonifay was celebrated as a wakeboarding **freerider**. He had a reputation for combining old school methods with modern flair. His style has led to winning every major wakeboarding title.

Parks Bonifay Career Achievements

Invented tricks called the Blind Judge, Crow Mobe, Temper Tantrum, and the Vulcan

1999: First wakeboard rider to land a 1080

2006: Only wakeboard rider to land a Double Back-Mobe behind boat (off Double-Up)

5x Pro Wakeboard Tour Overall Champion (1996, 1998, 2001, 2003, 2004)

2x X Games Gold Medalist (1996, 1999)

2x Masters Champion (1999, 2002)

2007: Wake Awards – The Legend Award

2004: Wake Awards – Best Wakeboarder

Parks Bonifay performed an "S-Bend" trick during the 2001 X Games in Philadelphia, Pennsylvania.

Water games run in the Bonifay family. Parks' dad was the first person to water ski on his hands. His grandfather jumped on water skis in the 1940s.

Cool Story

The frigid Baltic Sea had just melted on May 4, 2018, when Erkka Lehtonen stepped into the water. The Finnish snowboarder was going for the world record for most consecutive hours wakeboarding by cable. Lehtonen had plenty of motivation to stay upright. The Baltic Sea was a chilly 46 degrees Fahrenheit (7.8 degrees Celsius).

The wakeboarding cable was powered by solar panels, but they couldn't heat the water. After nearly four hours, Lehtonen fell down. He could either reset or call it a day.

"When I fell to the water, I felt disappointed," he said. "But positive and determinate attitude takes you far."

The cold water couldn't discourage Lehtonen for long. He decided to keep going and got back on the board. Determined, he stayed upright for 10 hours and 15 minutes. He beat the record just after sunset as onlookers cheered. Lehtonen capped off his record with a backflip and a selfie photo.

The Long Way

Lehtonen's record was broken in 2019 when Harrison Woodward rode on his wakeboard for 10 hours and 18 minutes. His dad, David, was just two minutes behind. Woodward's record attempt was a charitable effort for Multiple Sclerosis (MS).

"People living with MS can face challenges every day and regularly have to push themselves to the limit of their abilities," David said. "It is a tribute to the inner strength of everyone living with MS."

Non-Stop Wakeboarding Records

Harrison Woodward (10 hours, 18 minutes, 27 seconds)

David Woodward (10 hours, 16 minutes)

Errka Lehtonen (10 hours, 15 minutes)

Wakeboarding is a cross between waterskiing and surfing. A boarder holds a cable and is towed by a boat while "surfing" the waves made by the boat.

Surf's Up

Kelly Slater is the world's greatest surfer, period. Slater led a generation of surfers who brought the sport into the 21st century. He's claimed every major surfing title during a 30-year career. Simply put, Kelly hates to lose.

"When you get second (place)," he said, "you get hungry."

Slater began surfing at age 5 and turned pro when he was 18. Two years later, he became the youngest surfer to win a World Title. Although known as the world's best surfer, Slater has pursued many other interests. He's been an actor, a musician, a businessman, and an activist.

Above all, he's a winner. At age 39, Slater made history as the oldest surfer to win a World Title. He's won a record five straight men's championships and earned 55 Championship Tour titles. His pro victory rate is almost 75 percent.

The surfing legend isn't finished. Slater has no plans to retire any time soon. He doesn't have to travel far to find a perfect wave. Slater owns homes in surfing hot spots around the world.

Kelly Slater Records

5 straight world titles

55 Championship Tour titles

First surfer to earn two perfect scores under World Surfing League scoring system

Most Men's Surfing World Titles

1. Kelly Slater: 11

2. Mark Richards: 4

3 (tie). Tom Curren and Andy Irons: 3

Kelly Slater mastered a wave at the Samsung Galaxy ASP Men's World Championship Tour on September 16, 2014.

Kelly is the founder of the Kelly Slater Wave Company, which can build artificial waves far from the coast. This state-of-the-art technology brings surfing to those unable to travel to the ocean.

The Best of the Best

While growing up in Australia, Layne Beachley loved competing. She played tennis, soccer, and basketball. But she discovered her true love at just 4 years old when she first paddled out on a surfboard. By age 15 she was competing against boys, even if they gave her a hard time. However, they soon learned Layne Beachley was better than everyone else on a wave.

During her peak, Beachley set a record no other surfer, not even Kelly Slater, has achieved. She made history by winning six straight world championships. Later, a neck injury derailed her career. She considered retiring but returned ready to "surf with my heart and not my head."

Beachley earned her record seventh world title in 2006. She retired two years later. Today Beachley is a champion for women's surfing and inspires young women to compete in the sport. In 2018 Stephanie Gilmore tied Beachley's record by winning her seventh world title. Afterward, Gilmore paid tribute to the legend.

"It is an honor to sit beside you, Layne," Gilmore said. "Thank you . . . for setting the standard."

Most Women's Surfing World Titles

Layne Beachley: 7 (six consecutive, a world record)

Stephanie Gilmore: 7

Lisa Anderson: 4 (all consecutive)

Layne Beachley shot through the tube during the ASP World Tour in May 2001.

Making Waves

When a massive wave rolled Rodrigo Koxa's way, the Brazilian big wave surfer answered the challenge. Koxa had to maximize the moment; a wave this size wouldn't come around again.

That day, Koxa rode the wave of a lifetime. He set the record in Nazaré, Portugal, for the largest wave ever surfed. The enormous wave measured a record-smashing 80 feet (24 meters) high. Big wave surfers take huge risks. The rewards, however, are worth it for the surfers who brave the elements.

"I got this wave, and it was the best moment of my life," Koxa said.

Koxa nearly quit surfing before achieving his record. Several years earlier, a nasty wave in Nazaré crushed Koxa's body and mind. He lost the confidence and desire to surf. When he dipped his toes back into the ocean, he stayed away from big **swells**.

But Koxa worked hard to regain his form. By 2018 he was ready to ride the world's biggest wave. He'd conquered his demons and surfed into history. The wave, Koxa recalled, was nothing short of miraculous.

"I got this present from God," he said.

Surfing the World's Largest Recorded Waves

Rodrigo Koxa, 80 feet (24.4 m), Nazaré, Portugal, 2018

Garrett McNamara, 78 feet (23.8 m), Nazaré, Portugal, 2011

Rodrigo Koxa conquered a massive ocean wave in Nazaré, Portugal, on December 4, 2018.

Superman

Watching Blair Morgan was an unforgettable experience. His style of standing, instead of sitting, on a snowmobile redefined the sport. No one rode standing up before Morgan.

Morgan was an experienced motocross racer. But when it came to Snocross, Morgan stood out in a crowd. Morgan raced fast and had fun along the way. He even landed tricks during a race. His fans started calling him "Superman."

Morgan dominated the sport for over a decade. He didn't want to just win—he wanted to win by a mile. He tallied 84 national wins and won eight consecutive X Games medals.

But tragedy struck in 2008. Morgan was practicing on his motorbike when he took a bad fall and **severed** his spinal cord. He was **paralyzed** from the chest down. He retired from the sport he loved.

Morgan returned to motocross to advise other racers. But he couldn't shake his love for racing in the snow. He made a comeback at the 2018 X Games. Fans were overjoyed to see their hero compete in the Para Snow BikeCross.

"(Racing) was something I've been missing for the longest time," he said.

Blair Morgan flew like a super hero on his snowmobile during the 2007 Winter X Games in Aspen, Colorado.

Blair Morgan Career Highlights

1999 CMRC National Motocross Champion

1998 CMRC 250 National Champion

1997 CMRC National Motocross Champion

5 X Games Gold Medals (Snocross)

12 Snocross points titles

84 national wins

Trailblazer

During his final run at the 2018 Olympics, **halfpipe** skier David Wise needed to be perfect. Anything less wouldn't cut it. His first two attempts ended in falls. It was a disappointing performance for the 2014 Olympic gold medalist.

On his final run, he landed a switch double cork 1080, followed by a double 1260. Then he launched into a second switch double cork 1080, and finished off with another 1260. The judges awarded Wise a score of 97.20. It was the best run of Wise's career—and enough for him to once again claim Olympic gold.

Wise started skiing at age three to be like his dad. Freestyling later caught Wise's attention because he enjoyed feeling suspended in the air. He even describes himself as an "adventure addict."

Wise doesn't let his gold medals go to his head though. He uses his fame for positive purposes. He launched project Wise Off The Grid to encourage others to use environmentally friendly practices. He also wrote a children's book. During the 2017–18 season, Wise donated 10 percent of his winnings to charity.

David Wise Records

World record for highest air on a quarter pipe to banked landing: 38 feet, 4 inches (11.7 m)

Record for highest air on a hip: 46 feet, 6 inches (14.2 m)

Two-time Olympic gold medalist: 2014, 2018

Four X Games gold medals

David Wise hit some of the best tricks of his career to win gold in the Ski Halfpipe event at the 2018 Winter Olympic Games.

The White Knight

Shaun White needs a big room to store his awards. Pick any trophy in snowboarding, and White likely owns the hardware. Since his youth, he's been recognized as the world's best snowboarder.

Like many snowboarders, White started out on a skateboard. When he was only five years old, Tony Hawk took White under his wing to **mentor** the young star. But while White enjoyed skateboarding, snowboarding was his true calling. He turned pro at 13 years old. Older snowboarders saw a bright future for White. They nicknamed him "Future Boy."

White has juggled both sports throughout his career. He's earned 15 X Games gold medals in skateboarding and snowboarding. He won his first Olympic gold medal in 2006 in the snowboarding halfpipe. He took the gold again in 2010 and became an international celebrity.

Becoming the best has come with its share of pain. White has battled several injuries in his career. During training for the 2018 Olympics, White suffered an injury that required more than 60 stitches. But he recovered to win his third Olympic gold medal. As always, Shaun White took it to the extreme.

"I feel like I'm just getting started," he said.

Shaun White Records

First athlete to medal at both the Summer and Winter X Games

First snowboarder to land back-to-back double corks at the Red Bull superpipe

First snowboarder to win four consecutive gold medals in the Winter X Games SuperPipe

Three-time Olympic gold medalist: 2006, 2010, 2018

Most X Games gold medals and most Olympic gold medals by a snowboarder

Shaun White caught huge air during his gold medal winning run of the Men's Halfpipe competition at the 2018 Winter Olympics in South Korea.

TEAMWORK MAKES THE DREAM WORK

Mission Possible

In 2019 endurance athlete Colin O'Brady started **rowing** for the first time. Just a few months later, O'Brady joined a team of five expert rowers to cross the Drake Passage. The voyage would cover 600 nautical miles (1,111 km) from South America to the Antarctic Peninsula. And it required battling ocean swells up to 25 feet (7.6 m) high.

Colin O'Brady

It seemed like an impossible task. But "impossible" isn't a word in O'Brady's vocabulary. No motor? No sail? No problem for O'Brady.

His team began the journey in a 29-foot (8.8-m) boat. They worked in 90-minute shifts, taking turns rowing while the others rested. O'Brady's wife, Jenna, assisted on a nearby ship in case of an emergency. By day seven, the team crossed the 60th parallel, marking the halfway point of their voyage.

After 13 days, the crew saw icebergs and land just 9 miles (14.5 km) away. Finally, they reached the Antarctic Peninsula. O'Brady's team set several records with their achievement. It wasn't a smooth ride. The crew endured storms, snow, rain, and hail. But they stayed positive through it all. O'Brady's crew proved the impossible was indeed possible.

URURUGUAY

SOUTH
ATLANTIC
OCEAN

ARGENTINA

Falkland Islands
(Islas Malvinas)
(administered by U.K.,
claimed by ARGENTINA)

South Georgia and
South Sandwich Island
(administered by U.K.,
claimed by ARGENTINA)

CHILE

Cape Horn

DRAKE
PASSAGE

Scotia Sea

South Shetland Islands

SOUTH ORKNEY
ISLAND

SOUTHERN
OCEAN

Bellingshausen Sea

ANTARCTIC PENINSULA

Amundsen
Sea

ANTARCTICA

The Drake Passage lies between Antarctica and South America.

World Records Set During the Impossible Row

First row on the Southern Ocean

First row across the Drake Passage

First row to the Antarctic continent

Southernmost start of a rowing expedition

Southernmost latitude reached by a rowing vessel

Youngest person to row on the Southern Ocean:
Colin O'Brady, 34 years, 272 days

Oldest person to row on the Southern Ocean:
Fiann Paul, 39 years, 120 days

First ocean rower to complete the Ocean Explorers
Grand Slam: Fiann Paul, rowed fifth ocean

Most polar open water rows completed by a rower:
Fiann Paul, three polar rows

What's Up, Dog?

During his storied career, Mitch Seavey has proven dogsledding isn't just a young person's game. In 2017 he set a pair of age-defying records. At age 57, he became the oldest **musher** to win the Iditarod Trail Sled Dog Race, defeating more than 70 other racers. He also became the fastest Iditarod musher in history.

"I've never seen anything like this," Seavey said after winning. Neither had anyone else. Mushers of Seavey's age weren't meant to win the Iditarod.

The Iditarod is a 1,000-mile (1,609-km) dogsled race through the cold and dangerous terrain of Alaska. Seavey and his team of 11 dogs journeyed from Anchorage to Nome, Alaska. The dogs traveled at speeds between 10 to 11 miles (16 to 18 km) per hour. During his record-setting race, Seavey and his dogs battled temperatures that plunged to minus 40 to 50°F (minus 40 to 46°C).

A fan held up a sign during the race to encourage Seavey. It read, "Old guys rule." They sure do! After all, age is just a number, not a limitation.

"Fifty-seven used to be old," Seavey said. "It's not anymore."

In 1974 Carl Huntington marked the slowest winning time in Iditarod history. It took him 20 days, 15 hours, 2 minutes, and 7 seconds to cross the finish line.

Youngest Iditarod Winner

Dallas Seavey: 25 (2012)

Rick Swenson: 26 (1977)

Oldest Iditarod Winner

Mitch Seavey: 57 (2017)

Mitch Seavey: 53 (2013)

Seavey and his team raced along a trail on the edge of the Bering Sea to win the 2017 Iditarod Sled Dog Race.

The Family Business

Dogsledding has been the Seavey family business for nearly 60 years. The family has a motto: "Take care of your dogs and they'll take care of you." Mitch's father, Dan, moved to Alaska partly to participate in dogsledding. It didn't take long to pass the love of the sport on to his family.

In 2012, at just 25 years old, Dan's grandson Dallas became the youngest winner of the Iditarod race. In 2014 Dallas recorded the Iditarod's fastest time. He topped his record two years later. But the record only stood for one year when his dad beat it in 2017.

Dogsledding is a team sport that depends on Man's Best Friend. The musher relies on the dogs' power and endurance. The dogs look to their pack for comfort and security. From birth, dogs learn to trust the pack and their musher.

The Seaveys' dogs aren't house pets. They're co-workers. When they're working together, everyone is pulling toward the same goal. But dogs have their limits. Dallas never pushes his dogs beyond their physical capabilities.

Most Iditarod Wins

Dallas Seavey, 5: 2012, 2014, 2015, 2016, 2021
Rick Swenson, 5: 1977, 1979, 1981, 1982, 1991
Susan Butcher, 4: 1986, 1987, 1988, 1990
Doug Swingley, 4: 1995, 1999, 2000, 2001
Martin Buser, 4: 1992, 1994, 1997, 2002
Jeff King, 4: 1993, 1996, 1998, 2006
Lance Mackey, 4: 2007, 2008, 2009, 2010
Mitch Seavey, 3: 2004, 2013, 2017

Fastest Iditarod Winners

Mitch Seavey: 2017 (8 days, 3 hours, 40 minutes, 13 seconds)
Dallas Seavey: 2016 (8 days, 11 hours, 20 minutes, 16 seconds)
Dallas Seavey: 2014 (8 days, 13 hours, 4 minutes, 19 seconds)

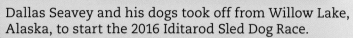
Dallas Seavey and his dogs took off from Willow Lake, Alaska, to start the 2016 Iditarod Sled Dog Race.

Master of the Track

Elana Meyers dreams big. She was a star softball player in college and graduated with multiple degrees. But in 2007 she felt she needed a change of pace and turned to the **bobsled**.

Myers was a quick study in bobsledding. She had to be. Bobsleds can reach speeds up to 90 miles (145 km) per hour! In 2010 Meyers joined Team USA for the Winter Olympics and took home the bronze medal. She was just getting started. She later won silver at both the 2014 and 2018 Winter Games and has medaled eight times in the International Bobsled World Championships.

With 11 medals to her name, Meyers is one of the most successful women to ever ride in a bobsled.

"I can't think of anything more fun to do than to drive a bobsled," she said.

Elana Meyers Bobsled Achievements

2009 World Championships, Silver Medal, Two-Woman Team

2010 Winter Olympics, Bronze Medal, Two-Woman Team

2012 World Championships, Gold Medal, Four-Person Mixed Team

2012 World Championships, Bronze Medal, Two-Woman Team

2013 World Championships, Gold Medal, Four-Person Mixed Team

2013 World Championships, Silver Medal, Two-Woman Team

2014 Winter Olympics, Silver Medal, Two-Woman Team

2015 World Championships, Gold Medal, Two-Woman Team

2016 World Championships, Bronze Medal, Two-Woman Team

2017 World Championships, Gold Medal, Two-Woman Team

2018 Winter Olympics, Silver Medal, Two-Woman Team

Meyers and Lauryn Williams
sped down the bobsled track
at the 2014 Winter Olympics
in Sochi, Russia.

Full Speed Ahead

Steven Holcomb raced to the max. A champion bobsledder, he aimed for "the perfect line, the absolute fastest way down." But bobsledding didn't come easy. Holcomb was diagnosed with an eye disease called keratoconus. His vision was so blurry that he was considered legally blind. Holcomb learned to drive a bobsled at 90 miles (145 km) per hour by relying on his instincts rather than his eyes. In 2008 he went through a surgical procedure to correct his vision. The treatment worked, and it was later named in his honor.

In 2002 Holcomb earned a spot as an alternate on the U.S. Men's bobsled team. He soon won medals in international competition. But his career took off in 2010. In the 2010 Winter Olympics Holcomb led the four-man bobsled team to Olympic gold. It was the first Olympic medal won by a U.S. team in 62 years.

Holcomb kept winning, earning two silver medals at the 2014 Olympics. In total, he won 60 World Cup and 10 world championship titles. Tragically, Holcomb died at the age of 37 while training for the 2018 Olympics. He remains the most decorated bobsledder in U.S. history.

"(Steve) was one of a kind," said bobsledder Curt Tomasevicz.

U.S. Four-Man Bobsled Gold Medals

Steven Holcomb, Justin Olsen, Steve Mesler, and Curt Tomasevicz: 2010

Francis Tyler, Patrick Martin, Edward Rimkus, and William D'Amico: 1948

Steven Holcomb and his teammates celebrated after their gold-medal winning run at the 2010 Vancouver Winter Olympics.

Holcomb was the first and only Olympic athlete to have a medical procedure named after him.

X Marks the Spot

In 1995, ESPN launched an event dedicated solely to alternative sports. It was a game-changer for extreme athletes when a half million fans attended the first X Games competition. The time for extreme athletes to take center stage had arrived.

More than 25 years later, the X Games remain the peak for extreme athletes. The summer games typically feature motocross, mountain biking, skateboarding, BMX freestyle, and surfing. In 1997, the Winter X Games debuted on snow-packed mountains. Skiers, snowboarders, and snowmobilers now had their time in the spotlight.

The X Games turned action sports stars such as Travis Pastrana into legends. The multi-sport athlete won his first gold medal at the 1999 Games and would claim 11 gold medals over the next 15 years. Pastrana shined under the bright lights. He became the first racer to land a backflip on a motorcycle. In 2010, the X Games created the Speed and Style award category. Fans gave it another name: "The Travis Pastrana Show."

"The X Games is an event but it's . . . still a show," he said. "I try to put on the best show possible."

The X Games became a global event in 1998 when the X Games Asia were launched.

Only a pandemic could stop the X Games. In 2020, COVID-19 forced the Summer X Games to be cancelled for the first time.

Most X Games Medals (summer)

Bob Burnquist 30 (14 gold, 8 silver, 8 bronze)

Dave Mirra: 24 (14 gold, 6 silver, 4 bronze)

Most X Games Medals (winter)

Mark McMorris: 20 (9 golds, 8 silver, 3 bronze)

Shaun White: 18 (13 gold, 3 silver, 2 bronze)

Youngest X Games Medalist

Skateboarder and silver medalist Cocona Hiraki (10 years old)

A large X Games logo stood outside the ESPN X Games 15 event in Los Angeles, California, in July 2009.

GLOSSARY

aerial (AYR-ee-uhl)—a trick that is done in the air

amateur (AM-uh-chur)—an athlete who is not paid for playing a sport

BASE (BASE)—stands for the four categories of objects that a skydiver can jump from, including building, antenna, span, and earth

bobsled (BAHB-sled)—a sled with a steering mechanism and a brake system used for racing down an icy track; bobsled teams include two or four people

bungee jumping (BUN-jee JUMP-ing)—an activity that involves leaping from a bridge or other object hundreds of feet in the air while connected to a strong elastic cord

free solo (FREE SOH-loh)—to climb a rock wall without using any ropes or protective equipment

mentor (MEN-tur)—to provide guidance and advice to someone less experienced

motocross (MOH-toh-kross)—a sport in which people race motorcycles on outdoor dirt tracks

musher (MUSH-ur)—the driver of a team of dogs pulling a sled

prototype (PROH-tuh-tipe)—the first version of an invention that tests an idea to see if it will work

rowing (ROH-ing)—a competition in which athletes move a boat with the aid of an oar

supercross (SOO-pur-kross)—a sport in which people race motorcycles on indoor dirt tracks

swell (SWEL)—a large wave with a long, continuous crest

thermal (THUR-muhl)—a column of warm air that rises from Earth's surface

READ MORE

Harris, Tim. *Triumphs of Human Flight: From Wingsuits to Parachutes*. Minneapolis: Hungry Tomato, 2018.

Hewson, Anthony K. *Shaun White*. Minneapolis: SportsZone, an imprint of Abdo Publishing, 2019.

Weakland, Mark. *Extreme Sports Records*. Mankato, MN: Black Rabbit Books, 2021.

INTERNET SITES

Red Bull: Parks Bonifay
redbull.com/us-en/athlete/parks-bonifay

Shaun White
shaunwhite.com

X Games
xgames.com

INDEX